New Age, Paganism and Christian Mission

Steve Hollinghurst

Researcher in Evangelism to Post-Christian Culture,
Church Army Sheffield Centre

GROVE BOOKS LIMITED
RIDLEY HALL RD CAMBRIDGE CB3 9HU

Contents

1   Introduction 3

2   The Death of God, Marx and Princess Diana 4

3   Is This the Dawning of the Age of Aquarius? 9

4   Returning to a Pagan Britain? 17

5   The Medium and the Message 21

6   Reconciled to God in Christ 26

    Notes 28

The Cover Illustration is by Peter Ashton

Copyright © Steve Hollinghurst 2003

First Impression November 2003
ISSN 1367-0840
ISBN 1 85174 546 7

Introduction

1

At the beginning of the twentieth century the philosopher Nietzsche famously pronounced that God was dead, and that we had killed him.

By the middle of the century the pundits were suggesting he was right. Sociologists and radical theologians were speaking of a secular world in which the advances of science and secular reason were extinguishing forever religious belief and practice. No-one would have expected that, as we entered the twenty-first century, spirituality would be on the increase and surveys would show that almost three-quarters of the population believed in God.

Since the death of Princess Diana, at times of crisis there has been great outpourings of public sentiment and the church has shared in being a focal point for this. Yet in spite of this church attendances are falling, even if the rate is slowing. If Britain has not become a secular atheistic nation, the spiritual revival has not been a Christian revival. What then happened to religious belief in the twentieth century, and how can Christ be proclaimed in the twenty-first within a Britain increasingly embracing a post-Christian spirituality? It is my belief that by looking at the rise of the 'New Age' spiritualities as natural expressions of our postmodern society we can learn useful answers to that question.

Can Christ be proclaimed in the 21st century within a Britain increasingly embracing a post-Christian spirituality?

This booklet seeks to do this firstly by looking at how postmodernity has helped a spiritual revival in chapter 2. Then in the next two chapters I will look at the New Age Movement and Neo-Paganism. At the end of each chapter I will offer a Christian response to these that can aid in evangelism. The next chapter then in turn seeks to look at how we can address the criticisms that these spiritualities level at Christianity as an important part of our apologetics in mission.

2 The Death of God, Marx and Princess Diana

Many will be familiar with Ellie Weisel's harrowing account of the execution of a young Jew in a concentration camp.[1]

As the others are forced to watch his death by hanging, made all too slow by his light body weight, one asks the question, 'Where is God? Where is God in this?' The answer offered is 'He is there, dying on the gallows.' This statement is not meant to be an allusion to the crucifixion; rather it views the holocaust as final proof that God was dead. For others of course he had already died in the trenches of the Somme. For whatever reason this century has witnessed the apparent demise of the Judeo-Christian God, or at least his banishment to some remote place beyond the universe where he, very properly, no-longer interferes with everyday life. It is hard to say whether the people who have left the church in droves were all once 'real believers.' We can certainly say that going to church has ceased to be a central part of British culture, becoming instead a minority pursuit of traditionalists who do not want to shop on Sundays.

For others of course he had already died in the trenches of the Somme

I am too young to remember the war, but can just remember Neil Armstrong walking on the moon. I remember at the turn of the century watching a programme using archive footage from the period looking at sixties' predictions of how life in the year 2000 would be. We were all going to live in plastic houses heated by nuclear power, wear wonderful 'no fuss' synthetic clothes, take holidays in outer-space, and never have to worry about illness since it had been eradicated. Forty years on, we clamour to live in old houses, are worried about radiation and prefer natural fibres. Space exploration is starved of cash and many diseases—once thought gone forever—are again claiming lives.

I can remember even more clearly watching the previously unthinkable spectacle of East Germans dismantling the Berlin Wall. It seems strange to remember that earlier this century many westerners with a social conscience looked to Russia for a new way forward for the world's poor. But long before the wall came down Russian Communism had ceased to inspire all but a few of our radical youth. It was also difficult to discern whether all this was a victory for liberty, human rights and western democracy, or for Levis, hamburgers and western decadence. The old dreams, however, appear to be dead, and only the gurus of computer technology seem to have a vision for the future.

Only the guru's of computer technology seem to have a vision for the future

In spite of the date of the millennium being set according to Jesus' birth, it seems that for many it was not a celebration of Christ's anniversary, but of 'the dawning of the Age of Aquarius' or some other 'global shift in consciousnesses.' The New Age is offering new dreams to disillusioned people, and whilst the numbers who would call themselves 'New Agers' are relatively small the prevalence of their ideas is much bigger. Aromatherapy, meditation, incense, crystals, astrology, eastern mysticism and various self-development techniques are all big business. Spirituality sells, even some forms of Christian spirituality, that is if they involve ancient chants under nebulous titles like 'Gregorian Moods' or anything claiming to be Celtic. It is fashionable once more to believe in something, indeed perhaps in anything, provided you do not tell someone else what to believe.

1997 was a strange year. The church celebrated the anniversary of Augustine's conversion of England, being careful not to offend those of other faiths. These, at least, took an interest in the occasion, in total contrast to the rest of the English population. Everyone else it seemed was interested in a far more important religious event, the death of Princess Diana. My abiding image of this comes from a programme screened that Christmas, aptly called 'The Shrine.' Among those filmed at the time of Diana's funeral was one of the many groups camping out in the London parks. This group had assembled a shrine, surrounded by glowing candles and at its centre a radiant picture of Diana. Next to it was another picture, a copy of an old icon of the Virgin Mary. I was more used to seeing someone else's picture in such a setting next to Mary's, but I suppose that just exactly *whose* picture had not occurred to the individuals who knelt before this shrine. Diana's picture was the one that seemed to belong. Of course such a response to public tragedy has been seen many times since Diana's death, after 9/11, at Soham and Bali as well as in smaller ways in many locations, but in some ways it was Diana's death that first brought this DIY spirituality into public consciousness. This is all very much in keeping with our post-Christian, postmodern Britain. It is the world of this Britain I hope to help us better understand in the following chapters—a world where the death of Jesus seems overshadowed by the deaths of God, Marx and Princess Diana.

Diana's picture was the one that seemed to belong

God is Dead and We Have Killed Him

Nietzsche is arguably the prophet of the postmodern age and for him the death of God was a key issue. As the twentieth century dawned God had been replaced by human reason as the source of truth and life. We seemed no longer to need God to show us how the world was or how we should live. Following the thought of philosophers like Descartes and Kant society had become secular, that is it divided objective public truth decided by reason and science from private subjective opinion, an area to which religion was relegated. Social morality became supposedly objective and ideals that once would have been viewed as Christian were now seen as humanist. Areas like education, medicine and government, once the province of the church, became areas for secular experts. In many ways God was dead, killed by a society no longer needing him.

In many ways God was dead, killed by a society that no longer needed him

If for many this offered a brave new world in which according to humanist ideology the natural reason of the human mind would draw forth truth and beauty unfettered by the dictates of religion, Nietzsche had for them a sting in the tail. He was adamant that the death of God was the death of the human project as a grand story of development in the way the humanists imagined.

The thrust of Nietzsche's argument was that shared truth and values required something to exist beyond human reason. The humanists were wrong in assuming that, devoid of outside influence, humans would naturally see life the same way. For him, in a world without a source of truth beyond human reason, there would be as many truths as there were people to express them. Of course for the modernists there was a source of truth beyond human reason—the natural order—but as Nietzsche and the postmodernists would realize we only knew nature via human thought and observation. Kant had suggested in his critique of pure reason that the order observed in creation was in fact due to the order in the mind of the observer. Scientists explored theories developed in their minds rather than responded to an order they dispassionately saw all around them. This enabled the modernist to see order and progress stemming from within a common humanity.

We were left with a subjective world in which people dwelt within their own reality

Nietzsche's observation that humans did not share common beliefs and values then ended a view of the world as a source of a single, objective truth. Ultimately the end of secularism lay not in the removal of the subjective, of God, by objective reason. Instead it was objectivity that had no future and we were left with a subjective world in which people dwelt within their own reality. Truth in both the natural and moral world became relative and subjective.

Nietzsche had something further to say about truth. If it was in the end purely subjective then any insistence on you believing what I claimed was true was, in fact, an attempt by me to exercise power over you. Indeed for Nietzsche this was the real basis of all social relations, politics, science and religion—the attempt to exercise power. For him everything in the end came down to what he called 'the will to power.' The essential trait of humanity was the desire to be top and to dominate those below, and conflict was the essential characteristic of all human society unless dominated by the strongest of dictators.

In many ways the Communist world gave ultimate expression to modernist atheistic humanism. Their dream was of a common society based on reason, but from the outset individual gain so often undermined the corporate aspiration. In the end the Communist dream would be eclipsed by the glittering prizes of Western Capitalism and the world of individual enterprise would topple the monuments of a collective good that had always required violent coercion. For thinkers like the post-Marxist Baudrillard the collapse of Western Communism in the late sixties heralded the beginning of the postmodern period in signalling the failure of the atheist humanist dream. This was finally to play out in the collapse of the Eastern Bloc a couple of decades later, the world of individual competition finally driving out that of collective struggle. Not that even the most hardened theorists of postmodernity expected all social cohesion to end, but they did predict it would shrink to small scale groups of people linked by common interest, ethnicity and tight geography.

Contemporary culture seems to be increasingly showing much of what Nietzsche predicted

Contemporary culture seems to be increasingly showing much of what Nietzsche predicted. People will often talk about something being true for one person but not another. When the experts issue their opinion we no longer trust them to be 'telling us the truth.' Indeed we may well want to know what they have to gain. Consensus politics is losing its attraction and fewer people bother to vote. On the other hand the non-voters are willing to protest over single issues in order to get their way over the views of governments elected by and thus supposedly representing the people. The post-Cold War world is plunged into conflicts erupting between different ethnic and faith groups and resurgent tribalisms and nationalisms.

The Gods are Returning

For Nietzsche the death of God and the one truth heralded the return of a pantheon of gods representing the many truths of a postmodern world. He drew inspiration from Germanic pagan myth with its heroes and war-like gods and saw this as a healthy source of encouragement for us to be like them and rise above the 'herd,' the common mass of humanity. Equally if we now increasingly live in a world in which the subjective is replacing the objective then the world of the spiritual, supposedly removed from public debate by its relegation to the subjective sphere by secularism, can also re-turn to mainstream life. This is why proponents of secular atheist modernism like Richard Dawkins find themselves increasingly perplexed and angered by the rise of supernatural belief in society when they thought it inevitable that it would wither away in the cold light of reason. Indeed it may well be views like his that have had their day.

Any faith that makes a claim to universal truth will be suspect

If the rise of spirituality at the end of the twentieth century was a product of postmodernity, then it also reflects postmodern assumptions. These emerging spiritualities are also being developed by an increasingly non-churched population who do not have a Christian framework within which to interpret the spiritual. It is not surprising that personal experience and belief, rather than tradition or reason, are the determinants of new beliefs and with that almost anything can be believed, provided it makes no claim to be true for anyone but yourself. Similarly in a world where postmodern literary theory tells us the meaning of the text lies with the reader, ancient texts of whatever religion have no authority over individual opinion. The emerging spiritualities of contemporary Britain are thus also strongly post-Christian in ethos. Indeed any faith that makes a claim to universal truth will be suspect, and Christianity is too readily associated with the old order. The elements of older faiths have instead joined new ideas and experiences on the shelves of a spiritual supermarket in which religious consumers select their favoured ingredients for their own spiritual recipe. It is the age of DIY spirituality. Indeed in many ways if the gods have returned, in truth 'the gods are us.'

It is the age of DIY spirituality

Is This the Dawning of the Age of Aquarius?

3

As I write we have been celebrating Easter. As ever this seems to be a festival the non-churchgoing turn into eggs and springtime and has little to say of Jesus' death and resurrection.

Radio Times' covers have often caught the public mood, this year chicks asking if there's 'a chick flick' on TV. Last year there was a bunny and an egg amongst the daffodils, symbols to do with nature and springtime and suggesting perhaps that Christendom has given way to a pre-Christian Pagan approach governed by the seasons. The back cover last year carried an advert for the 'mind, body and spirit' book club, 'the club that unlocks your true potential.' This was offering such titles as 'angel messages' that claimed to help you communicate with angel realms and fill your life with love and happiness. Or you could buy '10 steps to psychic power,' or a CD of Tantra that offered you 'the ancient meditation techniques of nomadic Tantric adepts in a beautiful and accessible form.' Titles drawn from across many different traditions and knowledge systems all available commercially packaged to empower and improve your life with the minimum of effort. In a world in which everything has a price and can be found in some marketplace, spirituality has become a commodity and a business. This market place spirituality is very at home in the 'pick and mix' culture of postmodernity and usually goes under the title 'New Age.'

Spirituality has become a commodity and a business

By its very nature New Age is hard to define and thus it is also hard to quantify its impact. However, what is not in doubt is the growth in New Age merchandise such as crystals, astrology, and indeed the kind of books mentioned above or of similarly named 'mind, body and spirit' fairs. But in spite of the DIY nature of much New Age spirituality, there are some defining features. Central to these would be what I would call the 'postmodern magical understanding' and an appropriation of eastern spirituality to a western consumer context.

Postmodern Magical Understanding

Western occultism and magical belief has a long history. From what we can glean, our pre-Christian ancestors believed in forces within the natural world that could heal, bless or curse and had wise people who were felt to be able to unlock such power. During Christendom this belief in the power of 'the wise' to manipulate supernatural forces developed a new form, based on Jewish and Christian mysticism that claimed to offer insights into the realm of God and angels and spirits. The magician in the western occult tradition became someone who believed he controlled spirits in nature, in the heavens or the very angels and demons themselves and could get them to do his bidding. Such occultism still continues but with the advent of postmodernity a new magical understanding has arisen.

It is oft quoted as an understanding of chaos theory in physics that a butterfly wing beating in one place can start a whirlwind somewhere across the globe. Whatever the strengths of this as a statement of physics it reflects a view of the world as interconnected. For the postmodern philosopher this world is also in the end the product of my mind. Thus by the same principle a thought in my brain can alter the world around me. In this way New Agers will talk as if one's thoughts had unlimited influence if one unlocks their power. So chants or crystals or symbols are not seen as possessing power in themselves or drawing power from a supernatural realm; rather they are aids to releasing the supernatural power present in all of us. Because the focus of such 'magic' is the subjective self, what works for one may not work for another. For some the key may be meditation; for others prayer, even prayer to Jesus; another group may find crystals helpful; and so on. You are simply invited to try out the range of products and techniques on the market and see what works. This approach also makes testing the 'truth' of claims to such inner power near on impossible. Things that happen as desired are seen as clear proof of such power whereas apparent failure is put down to either a lack of the right key to unlock one's power or a lack of self belief.

This approach also makes testing the 'truth' of claims to such inner power near on impossible

In the 1994 European elections the Natural Law Party stood on a thoroughly New Age ticket. As part of their campaigning they published graphs showing a fall in crime in parts of the Liverpool area, which they linked to setting up a group of 'Yogic Flyers' in the area who radically altered the spiritual atmosphere. They further claimed that if elected they would set up 7,000 such people across Europe and this would not only reduce crime Europewide but eradicate 50% of disease within 3 years, generate harmony between the EU's nation states and ensure a healthy economy. That the public were not convinced enough to elect any Natural Law MEP's should not deflect from the fact that they polled hundreds of votes in many constituencies and several thousand across the country. More, however, are willing to give 'magical' ideas a go when facing many of their own life situations.

The Consumer Appropriation of Eastern thought

New Agers often talk of ideas like re-incarnation and karma, and like Hindus and Buddhists, speak of all that there is as part of a universal cosmic consciousness. Yet what they mean by this is slightly different. Whereas karma in eastern thought follows from our actions in this life, for New Agers it tends to follow from our choices and our ability to 'take responsibility' as it were for our spiritual self. This was expressed well by the notorious case of Glen Hoddle declaring that disabled people had 'chosen to be that way.' If such people remain disabled then this must be either their choice or a sign of their spiritual inferiority. The desire here, like much magical understanding, seems to be to eliminate chance as an explanation of events, to push back the chaos of the postmodern void by creating spiritual laws by which to live in replacement perhaps for apparently failed scientific ones. If in eastern thought karma tells us all is as it should be, then New Age puts a postmodern consumer twist on this by claiming all is as I have chosen it to be. Monica Sjoo, a convert from New Age to Paganism, writes powerfully of how the logic of this approach to karma was played out in her son's death from cancer, which was seen as 'his soul's choice' in spite of his spending large sums on New Age therapies. As she notes

It is very convenient, is it not, for the white, privileged New Age movement to adopt the Indian upper-class Brahmin doctrine of karma devised to keep people in the caste structure and not to question it.[2]

In short, New Age teaching on karma justifies health and wealth as the rightful lot of the spiritually enlightened, and sees their absence as the result either of a desire to suffer or of spiritual darkness.

Along with karma comes an acceptance of reincarnation, but again given a New Age slant. This too is a matter of choice, and seems to rarely involve being anything but human. Past life regression has in some circles become enormously popular following on from this. Central here is what is often referred to as 'the self religiosity' of the New Age, its focus on the spiritual self coming to full potential and awareness of its divinity. The central cry of the New Age might be seen as 'I am god and so are you if only you'll realize it.'

Like eastern religion monism, the idea that 'all is one' is part of New Age thought. This seems to be given a particularly ecological twist. If I am to be seen as divine, so in fact is all creation. Much mystical experience in New Age is seen as connecting with the universal consciousness. At first sight this seems to offer an attractive affirmation of creation and of pluralism within a postmodern context keen to dispel the apparent exclusivism and dualism of its Christian heritage. Indeed, for the New Ager the spiritual reality is all-benign and there is no room for a dualistic 'spiritual evil.' However as York points out this leaves an 'unresolved dialectic between the idea of nature as real and nature as illusion.'[3] This stems from an attempt to take Eastern monism and make it a western materialist doctrine. For the Eastern mind the world is 'Maya,' illusion, precisely because the reality is that there is a transcendent spiritual unity behind all things. What many observe is that in truth this is what the New Age also thinks. Such a view whilst apparently divinising creation actually says it is an illusion to be transcended; and whilst apparently affirming difference actually denies it by claiming in reality 'all is one.' In the end western attempts to appropriate 'nirvana' may turn out to be pretty much like the cosmic void of post-Nietzschean nihilism and not an answer to it. If there are those who like Monica Sjoo have left New Age for Paganism because of the perceived justification New Age offers to the wealthy over the poor, others have made this journey because in the end they have realized that New Age does not inspire ecological action, but a turning from the physical world and others to the spiritual world and the self. Such views also make a mockery of the magical in New Age, as there is nothing in reality to magically influence. Magic becomes like a postmodern mind game in which I simply play with how I see a world that is ultimately just a projection of my own mind.

Magic becomes like a postmodern mind game

As the name suggests, New Age has a concept of a new era at its centre. In this it shows its debt not to eastern but western thought. The concept of the Age of Aquarius comes from astrology and the notion that the signs of the zodiac rotate into a new twelfth of the sky every two thousand years dividing history into twelve periods of two thousand years. That such a shift happened at the later part of the twentieth century, 2000 years after Christ, taking us from the age of Pisces to that of Aquarius is seen as no coincidence. New Agers thus often see themselves as the vanguard of a new world spiritual order to replace the passing Christian age. There is more than a whiff of Darwinism about this, combined with a tendency to elitism

New Agers often see themselves as having evolved to be the new human species in some way

12

amongst the enlightened, so that New Agers often see themselves as having evolved to be the new human species in some way. This also seems to fit well the New Age tendency to bless western capitalism. Indeed business training is a major area of growth in the New Age industry. In the light of the above it is perhaps not surprising that Osborn comments about such courses:

> Does this tendency presage a New Age transformation of the world of work? Ironically such courses may actually be co-opted by the structures of the business world to reinforce the *status quo*. One of the attractions of EST [a New Age performance consultancy] to business executives was its capacity to produce an aggressively self-centred executive with no inconvenient moral qualms about product, sales technique, or the conditions of workers.[4]

In summary, New Age has been attractive not because it offers an alternative to a postmodern consumer driven society exposed as working by the 'will to power,' but because it offers such a society a spiritual gloss that imbues it with apparent meaning. It deals with the tendency to meaninglessness and dislocation in postmodernity by giving us a place as the gods of a New Age, governed by astrological forces in replacement for the modernist concept of progress. It baptizes market forces and consumer choice as a demonstration of inner spiritual enlightenment. It makes palatable the 'will to power' as the product of the discovery of the true divine self. In short, New Age is an ideal religion for the western capitalist middle class in a postmodern world.

Responding to the New Age

Christian responses to such a worldview need to be thought through carefully. I would advocate the following areas of discussion in sharing faith with those in the much larger group attracted to New Age ideas and not just with 'hard-line' New Agers. In doing this I am not offering a blueprint for fail-safe apologetics, but some keys to open up an encounter with a God who in Jesus does offer things people are seeking and not really finding in the New Age.

Do Not Assume New Age Spirituality is All 'Not of God'
It is understandable for Christians to view many practices from the standpoint either of past occultism, and thus condemn it as satanic, or from a modern rationalist standpoint and dismiss it as nonsense. Either of these may indeed be the truth. I am reminded of the dual response to idols in Scripture as on the one hand laughable[5] but also on the other potentially demonic.[6] However, both views will make no sense to a New Ager and it

will not help one's evangelism to try and argue either point with them. From the perspective of the New Age such 'magic' is likely to be seen as validated by experience on the one hand, and coupled with a rejection of any concept of spiritual evil on the other. The biblical situation is slightly more complex than this. A good example would be the story of Balaam from Numbers 22-24. He is clearly a pagan prophet used to using divination and expected to curse the enemies of the king Balak, yet God speaks through him in spite of his occultic methods. The text hardly paints Balaam as a role model, but does raise for us the prospect that those with magical worldviews may encounter the Spirit of God and yet interpret their experience in magical terms. Indeed, if as those seeking to evangelize we believe that we are likely to find the Spirit already at work in the lives of those we meet, then such encounters with God by those searching in the New Age are likely.

Look for Points of Contact Rather than Criticize What You Feel is Wrong

We cannot expect to engage a person with a New Age style of belief on the subject of magic in the same way one would discuss it with someone who had a Christian worldview. Rather, it makes more sense to engage with the principles behind such an understanding. In place of 'magic' we can offer a reliance on God as the one who is involved in our lives in spiritual and supernatural ways according to his wisdom rather than and enables us to discover our true potential. It also makes sense to seek out in the other's spiritual experience handles on which to reveal God and show them that, after all, Christ may be what they seek. Experience of the spiritual can be turned to discussion of the way God's Spirit fills creation, or a telling of one's own encounters with God. Many are likely to view Jesus as a New Age magician and can be encouraged to reflect on Jesus' words and actions. In doing this Jesus' devotion to God and his service of others can offer a powerful and attractive alternative to the self-divinisation of the New Age.

> *Jesus' devotion to God and his service of others can offer a powerful and attractive alternative*

Avoid Adopting a 'New Age' Gospel

In Christian mission we share a world in which New Age is an attractive option and responding to New Age ideas, often expressed by those who are not fully involved in its practices but nevertheless breathe the same spiritual air, is important. One of the dangers in this engagement is that we too may find ourselves preaching a New Age gospel that seeks to baptize culture in the same way. Indeed I would venture that this is exactly what the 'prosperity gospel' is. When Jesus is offered as a solution to our life problems, as a way to health and happiness or as a means of finding self-fulfilment, is not there a danger of this being New Age and not Christian? I am struck in contrast by the emphasis Paul places in the Corinthian letters on weakness and suffering as marks of the gospel in contrast to the boasting of the 'super apostles.' I am thankful for the restored emphasis on the Spirit's work in areas such as healing—indeed I think it vital in our spiritually open age. But we must be careful here too that this does not became a Christian 'magic' in which the right technique replaces God as the source of prayer's outcome. Mission in this environment will require of us a good theology of suffering as well as healing and the humility to be 'clay jars' (2 Corinthians 4.7) and not wonder-working gods. Ironically it may be that whilst in the modernist secular world the miraculous was laughed at, it was precisely because of this it had missionary impact. In a more open postmodern world amongst the New Agers where the miraculous appears to be ten a penny it is easily interpreted in New Age terms and may be less of a missionary sign. At mind, body and spirit fairs Christians (myself included) have been right to pray for people and had a good response. However, many will simply be adding our prayer to the list of other healers who have laid hands on them that day.

Mission in this environment will require of us a good theology of suffering

Offer an Encounter with Christian Spirituality in Places New Agers Are

Those attracted to the New Age will be interested to engage with a Christianity that offers genuine spiritual encounter and a God who works in miraculous ways, indeed without such they will show little interest. Those who have set up stalls exploring Christianity at mind, body and spirit fairs have found people willing to engage on these issues, and I would commend this idea to others. Certainly we need to be taking our faith to them in their environment rather than expecting them to come to us. However, we must remember their response will be to adopt us with Jesus into the New Age unless there is more to our message. I suspect the key issues for building on such encounters will be ethical and not spiritual.

Find New Language to Talk About Salvation, and Explore Biblical Models of the Atonement in Addition to Penal Substitution

The gospel message of traditional evangelism has been about Jesus as God's solution to the problem of human sin and a world damaged by it. The concept of sin is not an easy place to engage anyone in a post-Christian world that has caricatured it as God telling us anything we enjoy is bad, and as a product of a world-hating and people-hating religion. Also the New Age has a strong self-centred streak and as such seems to justify much of what we might call sin. However, sin is also about things that concern New Agers, ideas of ecological damage and the image of God in people as somehow obscured and needing to be encouraged. At this level we can compare New

Age ideas of karma, self divinity and 'all is one' with Christian ideas of God's justice and concern for the poor and sick, the need to be transformed by the Holy Spirit, the reality of spiritual evil, human responsibility and divine forgiveness, the calling to care for creation and the making of each woman and man as unique in God's image. All of this can open up fruitful debate. It is in such conversations that I have found myself with New Agers having to wrestle with our own human weakness and with the possibility that their beliefs are not perhaps real answers to our condition or the threat to the ecosystem. In time this leads on to our personal part in such a world and the issue of my sin and the need to be freed from its power. At this point we can speak of the cross as God's way of identifying with our sin and breaking its power, the resurrection as the foretaste of our new life transformed so we are like Jesus and the Holy Spirit as God at work in us to bring about this transformation. As someone who came to Christianity from this type of belief I was a committed follower of Christ for a year or more before I understood any personal need for forgiveness. I suspect others will find this too.

Live as if What We Say is True

Finally, if the New Age has a tendency to spiritualize consumer greed, then it also challenges us on how we live. If we are to criticize New Age ideas because of their ethical outworkings with regard to the poor, the sick and the environment, do we live as those who care for these? It is not enough for us to speak of another way; we must live this out. Indeed it is not enough for us to talk about the transforming power of Christ unless it can be seen in us. This is also not likely to be a 'quick fix' solution, but one that requires an open journeying alongside people over time.

It is not enough for us to speak of another way, we must live this out

Returning to a Pagan Britain? 4

While Paganism has grown in this country alongside New Age many of its adherents see their beliefs as alternatives rather than as part of a whole, contrary to New Agers who tend to view Paganism as New Age.

Indeed Monica Sjoo is not alone in having consciously rejected New Age for Paganism. This difference lies in a conscious rejection of an otherworldly spirituality for a 'this worldly' one by Pagans. Pagan belief and ethics are essentially 'ecocentric.' The way different species are interrelated in the eco-system and mutually dependent on each other is seen as a model for human living with the environment and with each other. This tends to lead to a stress on relationships and communities as important over against the individualism of New Age ideas. If nature is seen as divine it is not because there is a spiritual reality behind it, but because the physical is divine. Indeed it is quite possible to be a Pagan and an atheist, interpreting the gods as symbolic representations of the diversity of the ecosystem and not as spiritual beings at all. For theist Pagans the gods perform a similar function, as revealing nature and not as beings to worship or placate. In this, contemporary Paganism is not like its pre-Christian namesake. Indeed many Pagans openly argue that Neo-Paganism is a postmodern invention using ancient Paganism as a symbolic reference point, rather than a return to a pre-Christian past. Others are keener to find affinities with a supposed British religion driven underground by Christianity.

Many Gods, Many Paths

Pagans will have varying beliefs about the number of gods but share an essential belief that there cannot be only one. The plurality of deity for Pagans affirms difference and plurality in life. Furthermore it is also essential that deity must have female as well as male representation. Indeed the female is usually stressed in a reaction against what are perceived as the mainstream patriarchal religions with their male god. There is evidence to suggest that many women who join Paganism come from traditional religions, especially Christianity, and are attracted by the concept of female deity.[7]

If in New Age the spirit world is entirely benign this is not so for Pagans. The gods represent death and danger as much as life and nurture, simply because these too are a part of nature. However, within this there is again a rejection of any notion of spiritual evil. Death and suffering are seen as part of life, not to be sought or praised but recognized in the end as an essential part of the way the ecosystem works. Pagans speak of getting to know the dark side, both as a coming to terms with this reality but also of the parts of ourselves that are destructive and dangerous too. However, whilst Pagans would reject labelling these parts of ourselves as evil, they do have awareness of right and wrong behaviour.

If in New Age the spirit world is entirely benign this is not so for Pagans

Confusingly this is sometimes expressed with a notion of karma, but not in the way New Age understanding does. For the Pagan this speaks of a sort of 'planetary justice' that means people get their just deserts as it were, rather than a system of choice or a justification of birth status. One common expression of this stemming from the Wiccan tradition is the law of three-fold return. This states that the good you do others returns to bless you but the harm you do rebounds on you three times over. This acts as an important qualifier to the overall principal of Wiccan ethics, the 'rede,' or rule, 'an it harm none do what thou will' which otherwise sounds too much like a licence to do anything.

Paganism contains many different paths or groupings and in some ways these could be infinite and there are many different ways of expressing Pagan belief. Many are not members of any 'path' but just do their own thing along with other Pagans. It is helpful, however, to have some understanding of the main groups. Wicca, already mentioned, is one of the oldest and most organized. It is sometimes felt to be too powerful by more independent-minded Pagans. Confusingly for Christians, Wiccans often refer to themselves as witches and operate in covens. This linkage is in many ways intentional as Wiccans are often keen to see themselves as the inheritors of a suppressed and persecuted religion represented by witches hunted down in the past by Christians and brutally killed and tortured. But it would be a mistake to infer from this that Wiccans carry out the sort of things witch hunters accused people of in the middle ages. Indeed the Wiccans themselves would agree with those who saw these charges as inventions born of fear and not based on actual events. Wiccans are however very likely to be practitioners of magic as discussed at the beginning of the last chapter. Another major area is Druidry, with several groups operating with a 'Celtic' feel. Others, under the name of Asatru, sometimes known as Odinism, work with a Norse / Saxon mythological base. These groups have differences but there is a broad acceptance that all are Pagans.

The Pagan Alternative to Capitalism

Paganism offers in many ways a counter-cultural response to western consumer society. The Pagans are likely to be amongst those protesting against roads and GM crops, against international big business and exploitation of the third world. Their stress on community and the reality of the world are positive and very much unlike New Age. However, there are some inherent tensions for Pagans. One of the issues that points to this is the fact that many are vegetarians whilst proclaiming that the eating of creatures by each other is a natural part of the world order and therefore good. There is a recognition that the gods are allowed to do things in myth that would be immoral for humans, yet their diversity is supposed to represent the affirmation of pluralism shown by nature and this is supposed to be the basis on which we live. This tension I believe arises from how Pagans view nature. They choose to view it as a harmonious interdependence of co-operating beings, but it can equally be viewed as embodying a rather Nietzschean 'survival of the fittest' that is definitely not what the Pagans want as an ethical basis. Indeed, Nietzsche would probably tell them that, like the secular humanists, they cannot have a morality that is not 'the will to power and nothing besides' without a deity outside of creation who acts as its source and guarantor. Whilst they espouse nature as it is, they seem to actually crave nature as it is prophesied to become in God's plan in the New Creation by such texts as Isaiah 11.

They seem to actually crave nature as it is prophesied to become in God's plan

Responding to Neo-Paganism

Many of the points made in responding to the New Age apply, the suggestions below are offered in addition.

Avoid Adopting a 'Pagan' Gospel

A Pagan gospel would seek to be ecological by suggesting there was no sin in creation or humanity, save that which is a blindness to our goodness and the goodness of creation as made perfect by God. A good example would be the rejection of 'fall redemption' spirituality for 'creation spirituality' by Matthew Fox. It is precisely this kind of belief that makes Paganism confused in attempts to deal with evil in the world and unable in the end to resist the challenge of postmodern nihilism and the 'will to power.' The strength of the gospel lies precisely in recognizing humans and creation are not as they should be and need redeeming, and that it is the redeemed world that both Fox and the Pagans really envisage, not the world as it is now.

Find new language to talk about salvation, and explore biblical models of the atonement in addition to penal substitution, especially those that talk of all creation being saved

The Christian message to those influenced by Paganism needs to be centred on the cross not as a symbol of world rejection but world affirmation—Jesus sharing in the reality of suffering. However, whereas for New Agers the resurrection and transformation of those who follow Christ is something easily welcomed, for Pagans this is a stumbling block. Pagans will resist any notion of the need to be 'saved' or 'transformed.' To counter this we will need to stress the continuity of the resurrection body and our current bodies as Paul does in 1 Corinthians 15. Similarly we must stress the continuity of creation with the visions of Isaiah 11 and Revelation 21; pictures of the fulfilment of creation, not its replacement with something totally other. Again concepts of personal sin and forgiveness will come well after grasping a notion of transformation as necessity for creation to become truly as Pagans want to envisage it.

Pagans will resist any notion of the need to be 'saved' or 'transformed'

Respect Pagans as decent members of another faith

Pagans are on the whole well intentioned; indeed to our shame I have found many of them far more caring and welcoming than some Christian communities. I re-emphasize this because some have wanted to see Pagans as Satanists, child abusers, black magicians and the like. Unfortunately they can look like the portrayals of such characters in Hammer films, but this is a false reading. Like all groups of people they have their weaknesses and their bad sides, but no more than any other group. Christians should treat Pagans with warmth and respect as they would adherents of any other faith. When this happens they are good people to discuss faith with, indeed especially if you are honest about the areas you do not agree with them on. Unlike New Agers they are not attempting to absorb Christianity into their own belief system and are often very clear about why they feel Christianity is wrong. They tend not to like the approach that 'all faiths are basically the same.'

The Medium and the Message   5

In postmodernity the adage 'the medium is the message' could not be truer.

If we are wise we will proclaim the gospel aware of what we appear to be saying as well as what we think we are saying. We might like to think that, as Christians, we define what Christianity means. But our society has decided for itself what we actually mean, and its conclusions are fairly negative. In secular modernity it was possible for the church to view itself as standing for spirituality and morality against the flow. It may therefore be a shock to us to realize in postmodernity those who are attracted to the new spiritualities view us as unspiritual and immoral, but in talking to Pagans in particular this is clearly the case.

Those who are attracted to the new spiritualities view us as unspiritual and immoral

The Challenge of our History

Part of the problem is the long history of the church in the West. We are perceived to be part of the established order, and that order has been racist, oppressive to women, and destructive of creation. Furthermore the church has played its part in wars, particularly the crusades and the wars of religion, and persecutions like the Inquisition and the witch trials. The latter is, needless to say, a particularly sensitive area for Pagans who genuinely fear the church in some quarters wishes to do to them what it did to their adoptive ancestors. We may protest that such actions were not truly Christian but if we are to be believed we must be prepared to repent for what the church has been part of and to be part of restoring the damage done today. In the end many people will need to see us living differently from some of our Christian predecessors before they will be open to the gospel.

If Christianity appears unspiritual this, too, may be a product of history. We have lived in a world that doubted the spiritual and this has I suspect led to an embarrassment about it in the church. We have perhaps sometimes appeared to be a non-spiritual society for the promotion of ethics rather than a religion. I am glad to say the signs of this changing are already present, both in the Charismatic movement and in the recovery of monastic spirituality. We must, however, not slip back into thinking that we must explain away the spiritual to a rationalist world; society has largely moved on.

But the problem with the image of Christianity, however, is not just one of history. For many our history is, in spite of our protestations to the contrary, a direct result of what we believe. This forces us back to look afresh at what we do believe and ask ourselves some hard, but I think necessary, questions if we are to remove barriers to the gospel in our age. This is the purpose of the rest of this section, particularly focusing on Pagan challenges to our faith.

The Pagan Critique of Christianity

If Pagans emphasize many gods and that there are female deities, it is partly as a direct critique of what they see as the Christian/Muslim/Jewish view of God, that is that there is one god and that god is male. For Pagans the plurality of gods is crucial to affirm diversity in life. A singular god is thus only likely to affirm one way of being and to rule over a monolithic, homogenous, hierarchical world. Thus, it is argued, it is no surprise that Christians have either forcibly converted or killed those who held different views. Further to this an individual god who stands alone is seen as naturally promoting the individualism that destroys the community Pagans seek to live within.

That God for Christians is 'Father' is understandable; it embodies the intimate relationship with God that is ours in Jesus in a special way, following as it does direct from Jesus' lips. But does this mean God is male? Most Christians would readily recognize it does not, that indeed whilst on the one hand humans are created 'male and female in God's likeness,' on the other God is not a human being with a gender at all. The trouble is this is not what we appear to be saying, and as a result many are rejecting Christianity for a Paganism that has goddesses as well as a gods.

Many are rejecting Christianity for a Paganism that has goddesses as well as a gods.

Christian belief in evil and the need for redemption sets a further challenge. How can the naming of evil not become a means of oppressing those we seek to see saved, or indeed not fall foul of the accusation Nietzsche would level that it is simply a ruse to gain power and that after all Christianity, too, was dominated by the 'will to power'? If the Christian story is to be, as postmodernists would see it, a 'master narrative,' how can it really not be an oppressive power trip even if it contains an affirmation of diversity?

Christianity is often accused of being anti-ecological and this is for two main reasons. First, the Christian concept of being stewards of creation is often viewed as a licence to exploit creation. Secondly, Christianity is seen as having a transcendent God distant from creation and a saviour who saves us from the world to live in a disembodied heaven after the world has been destroyed. I would add to this that I have heard several sermons to the effect that ecology is not something Christians should be involved in because the Bible teaches us God will destroy creation. Clearly the Pagans have a point.

Responding to the Pagan Critique of Christianity

The Trinity and the church as the Body of Christ as models of unity with diversity

The polytheism of contemporary Pagans only works if one does not live in a world in need of redeeming—otherwise their ethics require a source that does not affirm all options but exposes some as evil, *ie* a singular god. Yet is the inevitable price of following such a god intolerance and oppression of diversity? Are our only choices between postmodern Paganism and medieval Christendom? Christian thought in fact contains the basis for an affirmation of diversity and community that can still be firm in the rejection of evil. We do not in one sense believe in a singular god but one who is Trinity—not of course three gods, of which the Pagans would thoroughly approve, but a God who is three and one. Indeed, mission begins with God reaching out, seeking to draw creation into the community that already exists within the godhead. Such a Trinitarian God actually acts as a far better symbol of a harmonious creation as desired by Pagan and Christian alike than a pagan polytheism that affirms the destructive along with the harmonious.

Unity with diversity is further affirmed by Paul's image of the church as the Body of Christ

Unity with diversity is further affirmed by Paul's image of the church as the Body of Christ. There is one body but many parts, each called to be different. All are to be like Christ yet to also be their unique selves. In this the church is supposed to model a society in which all are welcome and all can find community. That this idea is lived out in reality may be vital for the church's mission.

True Christianity as a Rejection of the 'Will to Power'

John Milbank points out that Christianity often appears to be the antithesis of what Nietzsche advocates, indeed Nietzsche condemns it for caring for the weak and having a saviour who was weak.[8] For Milbank Christianity is uniquely 'the master narrative of non-mastery,' the one story that rejects the way of power for weakness, that has a king who enters to conquer on a donkey, who refuses to use force to defend himself, and wins by giving up his life and tells us to do likewise. From this perspective the 'crimes' of Christendom are not the result of monotheism but of a misguided attempt to use power to further the gospel when in truth it can only be served by the refusal of power and the path of the cross. That Nietzsche's 'will to power' tends to govern those who chose power is the lesson we must learn from the failures of Christian history. The good news for a postmodern age is that we have a God who in the means of our redemption not only overcomes the 'will to power,' that is sin, within us, but calls us to the refusal of power that is the only real alternative to a Nietzschean reality.

The gospel can only be served by the refusal of power and the path of the cross

Emphasize God as equally feminine and masculine
The Pagan option of god and goddess is not compatible with a Trinitarian God. It also may in fact oppress women by tying them to the gender stereotypes represented by goddesses rather than liberate them. However, the condemnation of God's apparent maleness is harming mission and we must take this seriously. In response should we as Christians also call God 'Mother' or is this to depart from our faith? It would take more space than I have to explore this in depth, so I can merely raise the question. However, the mission imperative is such that the burden of proof lies with those who argue it would be wrong to use feminine imagery for God and not with those who believe it would be right on the grounds that male and female are in God's likeness. If we are not going to use feminine imagery for God in worship and evangelism we need a very good argument as to why not.

The Christian faith makes us responsible to God for the care of creation
Viewed correctly, stewardship allows us to be truly ecological, because it makes us responsible for what happens to creation. If with the Pagans we view ourselves as part of a divine creation we must either decide that humans can 'kill creation,' and find ourselves with Nietzsche killing god, or we must decide that we cannot really damage creation as it is divine. This is what the often talked of 'Gaia' hypothesis says. Creation, it argues, will make humans extinct to save itself from us; in the end we cannot destroy it. Divinising creation may not prove a good motive for caring for the environment after all. The same problem is present in those theologies that seek to make God totally immanent or even evolving as part of creation.

God is bigger than creation but intimate with it
Many have mistakenly thought that transcendence is a spatial metaphor, and therefore suggested such a God is 'out there' and distant. However, God is transcendent in being bigger than creation rather than distant from it. In-

deed a metaphor that might sum this up well for a pagan audience would be to view creation as God's womb. In such an image God transcends creation but can hardly be seen as distant from it.

Salvation is not 'other worldly' but applies to our physical bodies and all creation

The Bible actually does not teach that we are to live as disembodied spirits but rather that we will be raised in new bodies (1 Corinthians 15). These bodies will not be subject to death and evil but will be bodies none the less. Similarly whilst this creation will not remain as it is; it too will be redeemed. Romans 8 speaks of all creation waiting for the children of God to be revealed so it can be freed from bondage to decay. Further, Isaiah's prophecy of lions lying with lambs also suggests a transformed creation not simply a transformed humanity. If the Pagans complain that we view the world and people as corrupt, our counter is that redemption is not from this world but of this world along with us.

6 Reconciled to God in Christ

> So if anyone is in Christ there is a new creation, the old things have passed away, behold, they have become new. All this is from God who has reconciled us to himself through Christ and given us the ministry of reconciliation. That is, God was reconciling the world to himself in Christ, not counting people's trespasses against them and placing in us the message of reconciliation. So we are ambassadors for Christ.
>
> 2 Corinthians 5.17-20a

In every age we are called as Christ's ambassadors. I hope I have shown that in a post-Christian world in which new spiritualities seem to be taking hold as the Church declines we can be confident of the gospel we have to proclaim. Indeed a gospel of reconciliation is very much the good news that needs to be heard. If in the face of the Nietzschean 'will to power' New Agers seek to spiritualize it and thus justify it, and Pagans seek to oppose it but do so by pretending there is no need for redemption, Christians can meet the unmasking of 'the will to power' with the reconciling love of God, the transforming power of the cross and the sanctifying work of the Spirit. If we are wise we will seek to do this without appearing to preach a God who opposes creation, denies diversity, is anti-women and in reality an excuse for the church to gain power. This will require us to find with Paul that God's power is made perfect in weakness, and that we are called to embody Christ in the church as a community of reconciliation, mirroring the love and community of the Triune God. We must also let our actions speak in harmony with such a vision for the reconciliation of all creation. We must join the Pagans in ecological action and in opposing the greed and oppression of a society in bondage to selfish individualism. We must also journey gently with those who seek spiritual reality in the knowledge that the message of reconciliation is indeed placed in us.

A gospel of reconciliation is very much the good news that needs to be heard

Further Reading

Paganism

D Burnett, *Dawning of the Pagan Moon* (Marc, 1991)

Graham Harvey, *Listening People, Speaking Earth: Contemporary Paganism* (C Hurst & Co, 1997)

New Age

John Drane, *What Is the New Age Still Saying to the Church?* (Zondervan, 1999)

Marilyn Ferguson, *The Aquarian Conspiracy* (Paladin, 1986)

Notes

1   Found in *Night* (Bantam books, 1982).

2   'New Age and Patriarchy' in *Religion Today*, vol 9 no 3, 1994, p 25.

3   'New Age in Britain' in *Religion Today*, vol 9 no 3, 1994, p 16.

4   *Angels of Light?* (Daybreak, 1992) p 72. EST stands for Erhard Seminar Training, a New Age self-development technique.

5   See Isaiah 44.9–20.

6   See 1 Corinthians 10.14-30. Paul seems to view idols as nothing but sacrifices to them as offerings to demons.

7   Research in America by Margot Adler published in 'drawing down the moon' Arcana 1997 suggests that as much as 70% of women joining Paganism come from committed Christian backgrounds that they rejected on these grounds.

8   See *Theology and Social Theory* (Blackwells, 1990).